Broken to Beautiful

Nelly Robles

ISBN 979-8-88751-177-1 (paperback)
ISBN 979-8-88751-178-8 (digital)

Christian Faith Publishing
832 Park Avenue
Meadville, PA 16335
www.christianfaithpublishing.com

Printed in the United States of America

y brokenness led me to you. I am thankful for my scars because without them I wouldn't know the Father's heart, and with my life, I will tell you of who He is. My brokenness led to my addiction. Brokenness was all I knew growing up. I was born in Chicago, Illinois. Both my parents are from Mexico, they came here for a better life. My mother had to walk through the desert across the border with my brother Fransisco Javier; he was only a toddler. When my mother crossed the border with my brother, the only thing she had to identify her to my aunt was a red rose. She had no money or any of her belongings, just what she had on her. She crossed the border into California; my dad waited for her on the other side with my aunt, his sister.

While my mother was pregnant with me, they moved from California to Chicago. I was a miracle baby. My mother's appendix was taken out while she was eight months pregnant with me and had to have emergency surgery. She had an allergic reaction to the medication and had complications, but the doctor would not deliver me just yet so he left me in the womb. A month later I was born on June 1, 1990. It was a rough delivery because my mother was still recovering from getting her appendix removed a month earlier. I was called the miracle baby in the hospital. My name is Nelly, and I was born in Chicago, Illinois.

I truly believe that the enemy tried to take me out before I was even born because he knows that I have a mighty call on my life from God for His purpose. I remember my brother Fransisco Javier and I had a close bond. I was very young, but all I remember is him and how he would play with me, protect me, read to me, take me to the store at the corner from our house in Calumet City on his bike and buy me candy. On June 10, 1994, the public pool opened, and my brother asked to go swimming with a few of his friends. My mom reluctantly agreed.

A couple hours later there's a knock at the door; there stood two of my brother's teachers from school. They told my mother that there was an accident, and my brother was rushed to the hospital. My dad was at work so we rushed to the hospital with the teachers. At the hospital I recall waiting in the waiting room with my mom, baby sister, and my uncles, my mom's brothers. A doctor from the hospital later took my mother, baby sister, and I into the room where my brother's breathless body was.

I'll never forget because I walked up to him, he had a white sheet over half his body, and I lifted it up and saw that he was wearing his Tasmanian devil swimming trunks. I stared at him for a few minutes and brushed his hair from his forehead and kissed him. My mother was crying hysterically and not just on that day. Her brokenness became my brokenness. Not only would I watch as she cried so much, but I wondered where my brother was, why he wasn't coming home. My dad was a drug addict, alcoholic who was also abusive to my mother, and I can remember my dad dealing with his pain in his own way.

My brother was not my dad's biological son. His father, my mother's first love, passed away before my brother was born. So as I watched my father drunk, I also saw my mom broken, blaming herself for my brother's death. As a child I was confused, I was sad. I had lost the only person that saw me, that protected me, that played with me. I loved my brother very much, and all of a sudden, he was gone. After my brother passed away, things were just never the same. My dad was drinking and using more and couldn't keep a job so my mom worked to support us.

Before my mother and father met, my dad was once married and had multiple children. Four of them came to live with us for a short time, three sisters and one brother. During this time it was difficult because of all that was happening. My brother had just passed away, my dad was drinking and using and not working, my mother was always working, there was a lot of fighting and arguing. My half siblings came to live with us for a short time due to physical abuse with their mother to the point where there were multiple hospitalizations.

During this time while my mother was at work and my dad had left to pick her up from work, while I was asleep my older sister and brother suffocated me with a pillow, and my mother walked into the room just in time. After that they were taken out of our home and put in foster care. Things just got worse with my mother and father. They fought more, he used more. One day I recall coming home from my neighbor's home and seeing blood all over the floor. My mother yelled for me to go back to my neighbor's home. Later when I was allowed to come home, my father was gone, and that was the last time I saw him for many years. I was five.

My mother became a single mom working and supporting me and my little sister on her own. She took us to a sitter in our neighborhood that soon became a nightmare. The sitter's husband, anytime she would leave their home, would lock my little sister and his son in a bedroom. He would lie naked in bed and make me watch porn with him. I remember telling him that I was going to call my father, and he was going to come and protect me. At the time I meant my earthly father, but not long after I said that, my mom stopped taking us there. I know now that it was my heavenly Father hearing my cries and protecting me from any further harm.

When I was seven we moved from Calumet city, Illinois, to Green Bay, Wisconsin, where my mother had family. We moved in with my mother's sister and her family. During this time of living in Green Bay from ages seven to nine, I was sexually assaulted by two different men many times in different occasions. I feared telling my mother. Not only did they threaten me, but I was ashamed. I believed there was something wrong with me. Why was this happening to me? I cried out to God. I grew up Catholic so I knew and believed there was a God. I had been dedicated as a baby and also did my first communion at age nine. We didn't go to church much because my mom worked so much.

At age ten my mom married my stepdad in a church. At age ten we moved from Green Bay to Fond du Lac. We moved to Fond du Lac because of better job opportunities, and we had family living in the area. I was excited to move away from where there was so much pain and shame in my life. The thing I didn't know is that it would follow me. We moved into a trailer home, and I was excited to have my own room. We lived a street away from my aunt, uncle, and three cousins. There was also a public pool for the residents living in the trailer park. I was excited to start a new school, I was happy to know that no one knew who I was. By this age I was convinced that people could see the shame, pain, and guilt that was inside me. I was already on depression medication and was seeing a psychologist by the time I was seven. No one knew yet about the abuse I went through while living in Green Bay, but I knew.

I started my new school in fifth grade. I made friends, but there was also bullying. It added to the pain and shame I was living with. I got called into the school counselor's office one day for the way I was acting out and not doing well in school, and that's where in tears I told her about all the abuse I had been through. She spoke to my mother, and I was forced to tell her some of what had happened to me. My mother blamed herself for what had happened to me. We didn't talk much about it afterward, but once again I started seeing a child therapist. My mom and stepdad worked all the time so we were going to family homes while my parents were at work, and there were times that me and my sister were home alone, so I had to grow up and not only learn to take care of myself but my little sister.

Both my parents worked hard to support us. My mother had nothing but the clothes on her back when she crossed the border with my brother, and now we were living in a nice trailer home that was furnished with what we needed and food on the table from my parents' hard work. I can't remember many good memories. Honestly, I remember pain, shame, and guilt. In sixth grade there was bullying, and I always felt alone. It was a rough year because though I had friends I lived in my shame. I was quiet and always had my head down. I was an emotional punching bag to other kids because

I would never speak up for myself. I would go home and spend a lot of time alone in my room crying to God.

I always cried and blamed God for taking my brother, the same thing I had grown up seeing my mom doing. I felt abandoned the moment I realized my brother was gone and never coming back. I felt abandoned when my mother was in such pain from my brother's death and worked all the time to support us. I felt abandoned when my dad left and never came back. Abandonment became a deep root. When I would lie in bed crying out to God, I blamed him, saying that if my brother were not dead none of what happened would have happened. I blamed God for taking the one person that loved me and protected me. I was buried beneath my shame—I mean what kind of child or person can carry that kind of weight? None. I was spiritually an orphan. I became the things I believed.

In the summer entering into seventh grade I made a promise to myself that no one was going to hurt me again. That summer I changed my hair color, I started dressing differently, I put walls up—a defense mechanism that I was going to make sure in my own strength that no one was going to enter. While in seventh grade I began acting out. I began arguing and fighting with my parents and other students. I wanted people to be intimidated by me and not mess with me. I was trying to make sure that I wouldn't get hurt again so I would hurt others before they could hurt me. I had no idea that I had a heavenly Father that I could run to and would shield me and put me under his wing. I was trying to fight battles that were never mine to fight. For we don't fight against flesh and blood but all spiritual.

I was dealing with so many battles raging inside of me. I tried many times to commit suicide with my mother's sleeping pills. See at school I would act all tough and bad, but at home behind closed doors I sat in my shame, guilt, loneliness, worthlessness, and the list goes on. I cried out in silence and in secret many, many times. When no one saw, Jesus did. Though I had gone to church I did not have a relationship with Jesus. I saw how big my problems, pain, and brokenness were and blamed it all on God instead of asking Him for help. And when He did help me, I did not see it as God, I saw it as luck. I did not glorify God nor praise him.

Though I was faithless, He was faithful. He never left me nor forsook me. When I was thirteen, my mother owned a restaurant, and I would work there after school. One night I was feeling sad and alone that I decided to steal some beer out of the fridge at the restaurant and instantly got sick. I didn't care that I became sick, I almost enjoyed the pain I inflicted on myself. I began cutting myself and harming myself in other ways. I was crying out silently for help. I believed no one could or would help me. It was like I expected people to know as if they could read my mind. I cried out in my actions, but that only got me in trouble so I started believing no one cared. For eighth grade my parents decided to send me to a new school, a Catholic school because of all the trouble I was causing in school and outside of school. I had already been in jail for fighting and on supervision. It only got worse for me there.

Though I made friends I thought so low of myself that I always believed they were judging me for everything. I believed I didn't have the right clothes so I had my mom buy me certain brands, but that didn't help. I still felt unworthy or not good enough. I believed I wasn't skinny enough, then started an eating disorder. My friends were wealthy, so I felt ashamed because I lived in a trailer, and they lived in mansions with nice cars and nice things. One thing I did do that I wanted to do growing up was play basketball. I joined the basketball team and played with my friends even though I wasn't very good.

During my eighth grade year at my new school, I began hanging out with a group of older kids from my old school. I began drinking on the weekends but smoking weed every day. One night I was at a party with friends my age from my old school and older kids; we were smoking marijuana and drinking. I was thirteen. That night I drank over the limit and smoked to the point where I blacked out. I woke up barely with a sixteen-year-old male on top of me. I couldn't speak or move. I blacked right back out. He had raped me, took my innocence, and left me in my front yard for my mother to find me. It caused me more pain and shame. I didn't understand, and my shame was too heavy to talk to someone about it. For my freshmen year I went back to public school. I was smoking and drinking more, skipping school, running away; I did not care about anything especially myself.

The summer after my freshman year I stayed with my cousin and her family in Green Bay. I met a young man. He was eighteen, I was fifteen. We hung out that summer and continued talking on the phone when I went back home. In October of 2005 I became pregnant with his child after spending one evening with him behind my parents back. I was a sophomore in high school; my life would never be the same. I stopped drinking and smoking or doing anything. I became very depressed and believed my future was over. I considered adoption and my aunt and uncle said they would adopt him. But in my heart I wanted to keep him, so that I did.

Anthony was born June 29, 2006, I was sixteen. When he was six months old, I dropped out of my junior year and went to live with his dad in Green Bay. I moved in with his dad and two uncles. His dad worked third shift and slept mostly all day. During the day while he slept, me and Anthony would stay in our bedroom unless I came out to cook or clean or use the bathroom. His dad did not like me leaving the house with Anthony unless it was in his company. There were times when he allowed me to leave with my cousin, but we could not leave without his permission.

We ended up getting our own apartment. Things only got worse. He became verbally and physically abusive and did not allow us to leave the apartment without him. He was very jealous and believed I was seeing other men. The abuse became too much. While he was at work, a few of my high school friends came and picked me and Anthony up from Green Bay, and I never looked back.

I moved back in with my parents and went back to school. I placed Anthony in a child's daycare right where I was finishing high school. At age seventeen I got myself a waitressing job for after school. My parents started helping me a lot with childcare. While working at a bar and grill I began meeting people and partying. I was drinking and using multiple drugs. My priorities changed, and I went from being responsible to believing that I deserved to enjoy myself because

I had missed out on so much. I missed my high school prom and being a teenager. I blamed everything and everyone.

I graduated high school and got my own apartment with Anthony. I wanted to be independent. I started college right after graduating high school for criminal justice. During this time I was sober. At age nineteen while in college someone I was dating introduced me to opiates. I used them for a short time and got sober again when I left that relationship due to trouble that we both got involved in due to our addiction. During the time that I felt like I was back on the right track I met someone. He was also a recovering addict which was not at all a good idea to get involved with. But I believed I was good, I got this, my pride was always in the way of me asking for help or advice. I had been shut down or been given advice that only ended up in more pain that I was afraid to ask anyone for anything. I was relying on my own understanding and did not trust anyone.

We started off as friends because by now I had my walls pretty high, and I honestly was not looking to be in a relationship. I was actually pretty happy with where I was at the time. I was working, going to college, and lived in an apartment with my son Anthony, and I was sober. Things were looking up when I met Kevin. Kevin was not my type honestly, so I wasn't really interested in a relationship at first. But he was so kind and treated me well and with respect. Not only was he a good guy to me, he was good to Anthony once I allowed them to meet, which was not right away. Kevin and I became good friends and spent a lot of time together.

We both didn't have a significant time sober and both relapsed. Our addiction actually brought us closer together, and we became each other's security. After a few months Kevin moved in with me and Anthony. We were both functioning addicts who worked, paid the bills, supported our addiction, and made sure Anthony was always taken care of first. Our relationship was doing so well until our addiction became first. We were always arguing behind closed doors about drugs or money. Truly I know now that it was not at all the drugs or money that made us argue. There was a much deeper issue in both of us.

The chains and bondage of addiction had us slaves to sin. The addiction was only the surface of what was really going on inside. When you are in active addiction you are blind to everything. We blame everyone else because our pain, shame, guilt, and everything else is too heavy for us to carry, especially on our own. But at the time I didn't know Jesus. I truly had so much anger and resentment towards Kevin. Now that I know the Truth, it was not against flesh and blood I was fighting with but spiritual. We were both blind and broken. But by now I had become codependent on him.

Though he had done so much hurt to me by manipulating, lying, stealing money and items from me and Anthony and pawning them, I stayed in the relationship. I believed I could not live without him by now, I had put so much into the relationship that I didn't want to leave it. He knew me so well, and I was so comfortable with him. I had a fear to open my heart again to another person. I was so vulnerable, and all I had was brokenness to offer. He knew that and was in a relationship, truly I believed this is it—no other man is going to want me like he does, and he knows basically everything about me. Plus I believed I could change him.

There were many times where I had to be the stronger person. I was there for him, so I believed that he would see that and want to change, especially when I threatened to leave him. That was not the case, yes, he would be great for days maybe weeks at the most, but the addiction and sin dug a deeper hole for us. He had been with me through tough times, and good times and Anthony loved him. So I stayed, but my guard went up. I did not trust him. Trust is very difficult to get back. Trusting someone means being vulnerable and opening your heart. This brings us to 2 Kings 4:8–37 (NIV), the powerful passage of "The Shunammite's Son Restored to Life." In reading the passage and allowing the Holy Spirit to speak to me I see that she, who is not named, is a great woman.

Her and her husband did not have a child, and though not mentioned, I believe she prayed for many years for a child. When God had not blessed her with a child, she lost hope and stopped praying. This passage tells me she had a good heart. In 2 Kings 4:8 it says, "One day Elisha went to Shunem. And a well-to-do woman was there, who urged him to stay for a meal. So whenever he came by, he stopped there to eat." She is mentioned as a "well-to-do woman." She urged him to stay for a meal; this tells me she is caring and is willing to open her home to feed and give rest to Elisha, the prophet of God. I truly don't believe she was looking to receive anything in return from Elisha. She truly had a genuine heart. She even mentioned to her husband in 2 Kings 4:9–10, "I know that this man who comes our way is a holy man of God. Let's make a small room on the roof and put in it a bed and table, a chair and a lamp for him. Then he can stay there whenever he comes to us." This shows me the kind of heart she had to be willing to do this for Elisha the Prophet.

In 2 Kings 4:13–17, "Elisha said to him [his servant Gehazi] 'Tell her, "You have gone to all this trouble for us. Now what can be done for you? Can we speak on your behalf to the king or the commander of the army?"' She replied, "I have a home among my own people." This spoke to me that she was in need of nothing. She was comfortable living the way she was, she had enough. But it is important to see in these scriptures that she was "comfortable."

When we are comfortable in life we stay there, we believe that this is good enough. But God doesn't want us to stay there. He has a storage room so big of gifts, hidden treasures—treasures that we keep close to our heart. She was comfortable, she had stopped praying for a child. She didn't want to open her heart to disappointments. When we hope, that's what we do, we open our heart to disappointments; so we get comfortable. But God's plans always prosper. Elisha doesn't give up because in 2 Kings 4:14, Gehazi said, "She has no son, and her husband is old." This scripture is so powerful to me because it tells me that God put it in their heart to ask him for a son for her. Our heavenly Father knows our hearts and wants us to continue to ask him for our desires, wants, and needs. But she had stopped praying so God put it in their heart to pray for her.

In 2 Kings 4:15–17 it says, "Then Elisha said, 'call her.' So he called her, and she stood in the doorway. 'About this time next year,' Elisha said, 'you will hold a son in your arms.'" How many times do we stand in doorways and refuse to receive God's gift or blessings from him? She pushes it away in verse 16, "No, my lord!" she objected. "Please, man of God, don't mislead your servant!" All she received was what he said with what she saw and knew. Her husband was of old age; she remembers many years of praying but not getting what she prayed for when she prayed for it; and she became discouraged and lost hope in the waiting. She said *don't mislead me*—how often are we there in our own lives? But God shows us He has more for us.

In verse 17, "But the woman became pregnant, and the next year about the same time she gave birth to a son just as Elisha had told her." This verse tells me that when we pray with others in faith, even if they don't have enough hope or faith in what you are praying, you yourself have enough faith God uses to produce greater faith in you and in the person you are praying for. Sometimes we may become discouraged when the Lord puts it in our hearts to walk up to someone and pray for them, but God wants us to do it afraid. Because what He's about to do through your prayer is greater than your fear.

The passage continues with the boy growing up, I'm thinking around nine years old, and the boy dies. In verse 20 it says, "After the servant lifted him up and carried him to his mother, the boy sat on her lap until noon, and then he died." Can you imagine holding the very thing God gave you and stopped praying for because of this very reason on your lap? What would go through your head? For myself, going to anything God gives me then dies I'm like, "I didn't ask for this, You gave me it, and now it's dead! Why give me something You're just going to take away?" But she didn't sit there and give up. She got up, laid the boy on the bed of the man of God, then shut the door and went out. She went straight to the one that gave her the blessing, Elisha, the prophet of God.

It's such a powerful passage as I continue hearing the word of God in verse 27 when she reached the man of God at the mountain. She took hold of his feet, and Elisha didn't push her away because he sensed something was not right, but the Lord had hidden the reason why from him. She says in verse 28 "Did I ask you for a son, my lord?" She said, "Didn't I tell you, 'Don't raise my hopes?'" I believe Elisha had a little doubt in himself because I believe God was testing him as well in this moment. Elisha said to Gehazi to take his staff and lay it on the boy's face. The reason he was sending Gehazi I'm not sure, but she was not going to leave him as surely as the Lord and himself lives so he followed her. In verse 31 Gehazi went on ahead and laid the staff on the boy's face, but nothing happened.

What happens next in verse 32 is so powerful, "He went in, and shut the door on the two of them and prayed to the Lord." The Holy Spirit really spoke to me in this verse because that's what God wants. He wants us to leave our problems worries, anxieties, fears, failures, addictions, all of it in a room where it's just the two of them and shut the door. God doesn't want us in the room with Him telling Him what to do and how to do it. She stayed behind that door waiting for Him to open it. That's what we must do: wait on the Lord, just as in Isaiah 40:29, 31. "He gives strength to the weary and increases the power of the weak; but those who hope in the Lord will renew their strength."

These verses show how true they are in this mother. She had to sit outside the door and wait, God gave her the strength and the hope, God-sized hope. God-sized hope that not only she needed, but Elisha. The Lord had hidden from Elisha the reason why. Our God is a manifold God—I truly believe that he was testing Elisha. The Lord tests our hearts all the time in situations and circumstances. From everyone who has been given much, much will be demanded; and from the one who has been entrusted with much, much more will be asked (Luke 16:48). The Lord loves us so much He does not leave where we are.

God knows what is next in our lives, and He has to prepare us, to lift us up to a higher level because that's where He is. The dream that the Shunammite woman hoped for and allowed to die, the Lord brought back to life—not once but twice. The one thing she gave up praying for the first time she was fighting for the second time. She had seen the goodness of God and His faithfulness. I believe she thought to herself, God did not give me what I always dreamed of just to let it die! No, I believe there's gotta be more in my own life. God can bring our dreams and hopes back to life every time. I had given up on my hopes and dreams from when I was a child because I grew up in my brokenness, the brokenness grew with me.

There were times that we would be doing well, and I would begin to trust him again. Each time I opened my heart to him he would hurt it. I opened my heart to disappointment. Each time I did it afraid but believed it could be better. But each time the very thing I was afraid of would happen. That only made me stay in that pain. I stopped hoping, and I allowed my heart to stay closed and hardened. I believed this was the best I could do or get, so I stayed and got comfortable in the relationship, broken and hopeless. There was a period of time that we were doing well and trying to get pregnant, but for two years I could not. I believed I could not have any more kids. Until we both got clean and sober, I became pregnant with our son Kamren at age twenty-four. When I was pregnant with Kamren something in me began to change. I stayed clean during my pregnancy, and I enjoyed being pregnant. I had hope rise in my heart again, but it was different. It's unexplainable. I had Kamren October 28, 2013. I was instantly in love.

Me and Kevin were doing well again for two years. We were renting out a nice three-bedroom home; we had a working vehicle; we both had jobs and everything we needed and more. He was a good dad not just to Kamren but to Anthony. During those two years of us doing well I was falling out of love with him. Our relationship started being more like a friendship with co-parenting, like roommates. He started using again, and I was ignoring it because I was comfortable. I was enjoying our routine and our neutral relationship. But it became really bad when he couldn't perform his duties and lost his job. I had money saved, and we began living off what I had saved and my paycheck. We were both broken so the relationship got worse. I was feeling used and taken advantage of. I was being manipulated and lied to. I was believing all the lies from the enemy.

I recently went through a lot of healing at Adult and Teen Challenge. I had to learn to sit still at the feet of Jesus and allow Him to work in me. I had deep roots of rejection and abandonment that He has healed me from. That doesn't mean that I won't ever feel rejected or abandoned. It means that they become weeds and those weeds need to get taken out before they become roots. Now that I have a firm foundation in Christ, the Holy Spirit quickly makes me aware of things in my heart I otherwise would not know of.

Healing takes time and commitment. It may not seem like anything happens, until later when you are in a situation where you would normally feel rejected but don't. You see the glory of God and the work that the Holy Spirit did within you. You will have to work with God toward your healing. To receive healing, you must make a commitment to God and to His Word. In order to do that you must be willing to invest your time to becoming a good student of the Word. If you do that, I promise that gradually, little by little, you will change. I spent a year at Adult and Teen challenge, and truly I couldn't have done it without Jesus. I wanted to share a little about my life and parts of my brokenness.

Truly to share the entireness of my brokenness would take me years. Jesus saved my life many times from overdoses before I even knew who He was. My addiction was always the solution to my problems. I never wanted to face them. Using drugs or alcohol meant I didn't have to think about it. I was avoiding things in my life that I did not want to face by using drugs. While using and avoiding my life seemed manageable, and I was happy being there. So the times Kevin and I were doing well, I mean that as in we were avoiding everything. We only confronted the things we knew how to handle. My thoughts were the biggest issue. Thoughts lead to actions, and my thoughts were always negative and superficial, not practical. I always wanted better but never knew how to grasp it. I've told you a little about my life externally, but what was inward was a result from that and more.

Before I met Jesus on May 18, 2021, I was independent but codependent, and what I mean is on the inside of me I truly thought I could do everything myself; I don't need anyone. I was too prideful to ask for help. I was ashamed of needing help, and I would feel guilty for asking for help. The enemy really kept me in that bondage for as long as I could remember. I grew into it, it molded me. I had been hurt by men, and I did not want to need them. I didn't want to attach myself to someone that I knew was going to hurt me. I believed it. The mind is so powerful that because I believed I was going to get hurt, that's exactly what I got. What you set your mind on is what you will manifest. I've been in four relationships, and all four triggered deep pain that was already there.

At the time I didn't see it that way. I was blind and broken. All I saw was brokenness. Jesus says in Luke 11:34–35, "Your eye is the lamp of your body. When your eyes are healthy, your whole body also is full of light. But when they are unhealthy, your body also is full of darkness. See to it, then, that the light within you is not darkness." That's so powerful and true. My light within me was darkness, so what I saw was darkness.

Jesus has to first cleanse you from all that darkness in our hearts and replace them with Truth. For me it took a year at Adult and Teen challenge. I had to go through many trials. Trials brought things out of me that I did not see or were aware of because I was living in darkness. The Holy Spirit will bring darkness to light. How you respond to it is your choice. My choice was first to cry in a quiet room with Jesus. Adult and Teen Challenge is a safe place to just focus on allowing Jesus to heal your heart. So I cried and asked Jesus for help. As I'm crying looking at myself and the choices I made I'd ask the Holy Spirit, "Why do I do these things? I don't want to be like this. Please help me change." How did I get to Adult and Teen challenge you may ask. God.

God has a plan for us for a much greater purpose. I didn't believe I had a purpose before Jesus entered my life. I had become extremely depressed after breaking the relationship with Kevin. I wanted to break up the relationship for many years, but fear had stopped me. I thought and believed I needed him to help me with Kamren and Anthony. I believed that no man in the world will ever want to be with me—I have nothing, I am nothing, and I am a single mother of two boys. Those are lies from the enemy that I could not see, I was blinded because all I saw was what I didn't have and who I was in that moment.

Broken as I was, I was not in a position to even be in a relationship because I would only attract other broken people and the more we put ourselves in broken relationships, the more we believe we are unworthy and hopeless. We look at the relationship to validate us. That's what I did. I looked to others for my worth. I've learned now that when we do that, it's only temporary satisfaction. We go to the wrong well for water when we are thirsty; and that water being compliments, praise, and flattery from people that they can easily take back. For example, a nice-looking young man tells you you're beautiful, but the minute you don't say or do what he needs to make himself feel better, he takes that compliment back and calls you ugly.

That thirst for compliments makes you thirsty for more. You start needing and wanting them to make you feel better, but you are still left empty. Jesus never has or will take His word back. When Jesus says you are free, you are free indeed. Jesus says you're worth dying for—that makes you worthy. Jesus is the well we need to run to and the water that gives us life, eternal life. He really spoke to me in times of prayer and reading John 4. I'm in a season where God wants me to be content with myself. I had about two weeks of being consumed with social media and validation from others before I listened to the Lord. I was feeling alone. When I did, I would talk to a male friend, trying to fill a hole that only Jesus can.

One thing that I desire in my life is to get married, and truly I had lost hope of ever getting married, but the Lord put that desire in my heart. When God puts His desire for you in your life, He is the one that is responsible to make it happen. I'm only responsible to believe and trust by faith that He will do what He says at the right time. The thing with humans is that we think God takes forever to do something, so then we try to do it on our own and then it fails, and we blame it on God. God is never early or late. He is always right on time. God takes His time with us because He wants to prepare us for what He wants to give us. We may just not be ready for it yet. I can tell you right now that I desire to get married, but I am definitely not ready for it yet. The Lord is working on developing my character.

In the two weeks that I was feeling alone and trying to grab hold of something I can see to have temporary pleasure, for example social media and compliments or validation, I could see it and saved it so any time I was feeling a type of way I would go back to that message, and it would make me feel good for a second, but I was feeling empty. The next day I would start my morning in prayer and devotional time and worshipping; and I would have God's joy, peace, and love overflowing, until I went on social media and would share how great I'm doing by myself. I was feeling unseen and alone again. Each day I was seeing a pattern and the Lord kept showing me John 4 in different sermons and church, so I was like *Lord, what are you trying to show me?*

It wasn't until I got on my knees and prayed and deleted my social media apps that the Lord really got my attention. He had already been trying to make me aware of myself, but I wasn't having it. The Lord gave me a revelation about myself in John 4. The Samaritan woman had six husbands which the one she was living with was not her husband. Jesus wants to be number 7. What did God do on the seventh day? He rested. Jesus wants to be our husband and to rest in Him. He is the only one who makes you whole because He is whole. We are whole in Him. We are redeemed, our salvation. Jesus is the lamp to our feet when we can't see. We must fix our eyes on Jesus the author and perfector of faith. Apart from Him we can do nothing.

My depression and hopelessness led me to relapse February 1, 2019, and I overdosed. My boys were taken out of my home by CPS and placed with family. I was in the hospital for five days. It was a miracle I was even alive. But God's word says in Luke 9:27, "But I tell you truly, there are some standing here who will not taste death until they see the kingdom of God." His word is true because He did not allow me to die before seeing Him here on earth as it is in heaven. He is not done with me yet. It is written that God chooses what this world calls as foolishness to shame the wise. I am the last person anyone thought had a chance. But God stepped in and what you see now is a miracle. I am alive and transformed by the renewing of my mind. All I had to do is sit still for a year at Adult and Teen Challenge and allow the Holy Spirit to do what He does best. I had to learn in obedience according to His Word.

All my life I wanted something different, I knew there was better, but I didn't know how. I didn't know how to live because the way I was living was the only way I knew how to live. I didn't know that the Bible is life and love, joy, peace, and hope all found in Jesus Christ. I feel like I've been gypped from this secret my whole life. And truly it's not even a secret; people just don't like talking about it. God's word says to always be ready when people ask you about the hope you have, to share the gospel of Jesus Christ. Our culture and world do not accept Him, so they don't accept His followers, but Jesus says "I am sending you as the Father sent me." The servants are not greater than their master. Meaning if Jesus got persecuted, insulted, gossiped about we will too.

We forget that we serve a God who understands. He endured all of it, so we didn't have to. Jesus does promise we will have troubles in this life, but thank God for the Holy Spirit. Jesus said we will do even greater things than He because the Father was sending a helper, advocate, guide. He is everything we need. We are not perfect so many times we will fail and fall, but our Savior does not leave us there. He knows everywhere we've been, and He tells us we never have to go back, "Just follow me."

The day I cried out to God, I was at my lowest. I have been low, but this day, I was done. After my overdose, my addiction got worse. I was so broken that the only thing I had to live for which were my kids had been taken away from me. I was blaming everyone but really what I had was a weight of shame and guilt that I could not carry on my own, and we are not meant to. I was trying to fill the God-sized hole in my heart with external things. Not possible.

Jesus is the Way, the Truth and the Life. He alone can fill your heart because he created it. He formed you in your mother's womb. We are made in God's image, but the enemy and the world distorted it, and we allowed and believed the lies that we are not seen; that we are unworthy, unloved, and rejected. But the Truth is sharper than any double-edged sword. When the Truth pierced my heart, lies started falling off. God's love moved in and by faith mountains had to move. Mountains that were in the way of me receiving love. I had to learn how to receive love in order for me to give it. God has fully restored my family. The Lord has restored my heart and has made me whole and healthy. I am a miracle. I've been delivered from my addiction. I no longer live in bondage to it. I have joy in chaos and peace that makes no sense. I have hope and a future.

The day I cried out to God with all my heart and soul, I had planned to kill myself. But God stepped in. I was arrested twenty minutes later, before I had a chance to harm myself, and I just knew in my heart that it was God. This time I did not wrestle with Him. I hated my life and who I had become. I did end my life that day—I died to myself. I am a new creation in Christ; the old is gone, and the new is here. God prepared me at Adult and Teen challenge. He taught me a new way of life through the program. It's Jesus in the program that changed me. He continues to develop my character. I have to crucify my flesh daily, capture my thoughts, and make them obedient to Christ. It is a daily thing, a discipline that becomes a habit. Habits create character and that character destiny. Romans 8:28–30 says,

> And we know that in all things God works for the good of those who love him, who have been called according to his purpose. For those God foreknew he also predestined to be conformed to the image of his Son, that he might be the first-born among many brothers and sisters. And those he predestined, he also called; those he called, he also justified; those he justified, he also glorified.

God will have mercy on whom He has mercy, and He has compassion on whom He has compassion, Romans 9:16–17 says. It does not, therefore, depend on human desire or effort, but on God's mercy. For scripture says to Pharaoh, "I raised you up for this very purpose, that I might display my power in you and that my name might be proclaimed in all the earth." I am truly and deeply in love with Jesus. I have seen the light, and I never want to go back. The life I live now I live for Jesus because He first loved me and gave Himself up for me, so now I will do the same for Him. I give Him my life, I surrender it. I knew darkness, brokenness, pain, and death. To now being the light in the world in Christ Jesus to show the world His glory through me and my life. God created us for His glory. The First Epistle of Peter 2:9–10 says,

> But you are a chosen people, a royal priesthood, a holy nation, God's special possession, that you may declare the praises for him who called you out of darkness into his wonderful light. Once you were not a people, but now you are the people of God; once you had not received mercy, but now you have received mercy.

Who I was before was ashamed, unloved, hopeless, rejected, and abandoned. Who am I now? I am loved, chosen, accepted, and I am a child of God. My hope is in Jesus Christ. He will never fail me, and He will never fail you. The day God heard my cry and placed me in jail so I wouldn't harm myself I knew in my heart I was supposed to sit still, so I sat still until I had all drugs out of my body. Then God gave me a vision of me being a motivational speaker. I had this deep impression in my heart that I will write a book someday.

During my time at Adult and Teen Challenge I loved to write and study the Word. I was thirsty and hungry to know God more. My intimate relationship with God got deeper as I got to know Jesus more. Jesus became my number one desire and my heart burns for him. I wrote journal after journal of what God was showing me and what I was hearing in prayer and in his Word. I remember one week where the Lord put it on my heart to pray about this book that I now desire to write. I said, Lord if you want me to write a book, You will have to show me how, who, what, and when because I don't know where to start. And that Sunday at ministry in a small town of Wisconsin they provided lunch for us that day.

A nice man from the church we were at sat at the table I was at with four other of my sisters from adult and teen challenge. Close to us being done eating he asked if any of us enjoyed playing music. We all said no. Then he asked if any of us enjoyed writing, and I said I love to write. He asked if I ever thought about writing a book, and I said yes, and he went on to tell me how he's written articles and books, and I said God just answered my prayer. He gave me the information to Christian Faith publishing, and it stuck with me. He told me to write down the ideas and things God speaks to me, and I said I've been doing that this whole time at Adult and Teen challenge.

I graduated, and I contacted them right away. Praise God! I have a God-sized hope, and I know that my job is to believe. God's job is the outcome. He is God Almighty. He is sovereign. He knows everything from beginning to end. I place this in His hands. I pray that everything I say, think, and do is pleasing to Him. I pray that anyone who comes in contact with this book will be blessed and that God will use it to do mighty things all for His glory. I will continue to serve Him and share the gospel everywhere I go, sharing the hope that is in Jesus. Walking in love and in Truth as He leads me. I pray that God will open your eyes to see, ears to hear, and open your heart to receive from heaven, believe, and understand as He is a personal God. He will speak to you. Draw close to Him, and He will draw close to you. To the measure you put in is the measure He will.

Trust in him. Be patient. Walk by faith and not by sight. He is working in the unseen, preparing us for what is to come. Developing your character. Let your faith be greater than your fear. Do not be afraid or discouraged. He is with you and will strengthen you and help you. He will uphold you with His righteous right hand. In all things seek Him, and you will find him. The more He showed Himself to me the more I wanted to draw closer to Him. I want more and more of him. I love Jesus so much because only He and I know how broken I was. I truly didn't see light at the end of the tunnel in my lifetime. God knew otherwise. I'm in awe of God's love. I have never known true pure love in my life. And I'm so grateful God did not allow me to die before knowing. I'm thankful He knows my heart. I'm thankful I am fully known, and He still loves me. How is that possible? All things are possible with God. Don't set limits on God because He can and will do greater things in you and through you and I. Stay in prayer and know that there is better. Every time you think you have reached it, He will lift you up higher and show you more, and He will continue to do that until He takes us home.

About the Author

Nelly Robles was born again at thirty years of age, experiencing the call of God at this time and the desire to preach, encourage, save souls for Jesus. Nelly is a delivered addict who was homeless and had lost everything when, on April 5, 2021, hope found her. Jesus, the healer and restorer of our souls, found her and led her to adult-and-teen challenge, where He transformed her by renewing her mind through the work of the Holy Spirit. God put a strong desire in her heart to know more of Him. She has the heart of God and desires to help others to a deeper relationship with the Lord Jesus through her life and her experiences. No one is too broken; the Lord met her where she was—broken and covered in shame—and raised her up in glory with Him. She gave Him her garbage, and He gave her treasure. Nelly has a desire to help other women, to share the love of Jesus, and to do the Father's will. Ecclesiastes 3:11 says, "He has made everything beautiful in its time. He has also set eternity in the human heart; yet no one can fathom what God has done from beginning to end."

www.ingramcontent.com/pod-product-compliance
Lightning Source LLC
Chambersburg PA
CBHW022045150726
47990CB00004B/1624